Why Grandmas Go To Heaven

Written and Illustrated by:

Petisamaria G. Hall

AuthorHouse™
1663 Liberty Drive
Bloomington, IN 47403
www.authorhouse.com
Phone: 1-800-839-8640

First published by AuthorHouse 11/17/2009

ISBN: 978-1-4490-4962-1 (sc)

Library of Congress Control Number: 2009912320

Printed in the United States of America
Bloomington, Indiana

This book is printed on acid-free paper.

authorHOUSE®

I would like to dedicate this book to my three beautiful, inspirational children- Cydneyanne, Joshuah and Preston.

Why do grandmas go to heaven?
Well, here are a few reasons why.
Because, if there were no grandmas in heaven,
the angels would never fly.

Everyone knows that grandma mends clothes,
well in heaven, she makes the wings.
So the angels can fly, that are sent down to spy,
then fly back to tell grandma everything.

You know how grandmas songs are the very best songs,
well heaven needs her there to sing.
So our angels can teach us new lulla-byes,....

.... and our birdies will know what to sing.

You see, it really doesn't matter how young you are,
or old, or what you may have read in stories,
or what you may have been told.
Because heaven is a magical place, up there you don't get sick.
And your grandma is as fit as a fiddle, and no longer needs her stick.

They crown all the grandmas up in heaven,
she graduates life with honors.
For learning, and sharing, for teaching, and caring, and always loving others.

Now with all of heaven, and its glory,
your grandmas food is the best to eat.
Your grandma is the "main dish" in heaven,
so without her, there is no feast.
And grandmas cooking is loved so much,
she really cannot be beat.

Grandmas are great story tellers, as well
and heaven knows this is quite true.
Your grandma tells all, from winter to fall,
about special times she had with you.

Grandmas are great entertainers too,
she can make you feel ten feet tall.
Well some of the games in heaven, she plays,
and coaches Little Angels T-ball.

Hey, Heaven lets grandmas come visit us too,
more often than you think.
At night while you're snuggled down in your bed,
she's counting all of your sheep.

So, just in case, you have wondered "why",
have had a few tears in your cry, and you are sad because your grandma has gone and left you.

Have no fear, she's still here, it's just another job my dear, and she really just wants you to know she loves you.

So, do your best at what you do, because your grandma is watching you.

Brush your teeth, comb your hair, and clean your mess....

....and don't forget to study, for that test.

Now "Grandma loves you", please be good,
And eat your greens, just like you should.

And the very next time you here a birdie sing...

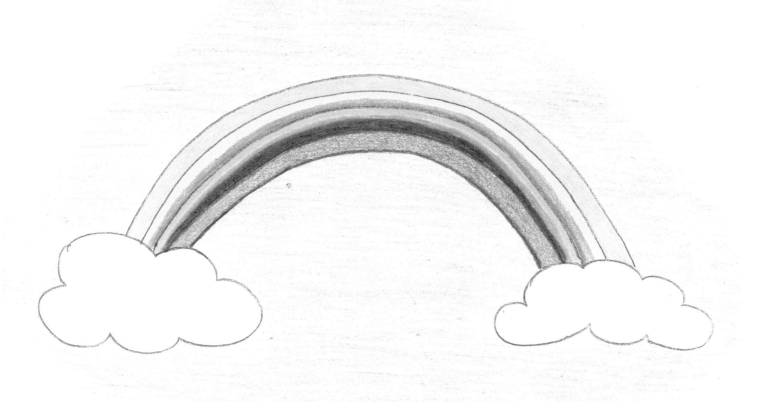

Or see a rainbow,

Plant a flower,

Or sing a "new song" in your shower,
just remember that ....

Your Grandma's still watching.
("Grandma loves you.")
The End.

This is a story about a magical place, where all our Grandmas go.
Your Grandmas purpose up in Heaven, and why she had to go.
A story of 'Why" it's very important to do the best you do.
Your Grandma may not be here anymore,
but she's still watching over you.

CPSIA information can be obtained
at www.ICGtesting.com
Printed in the USA
256508LV00002BA